PEARL HARBOR

The Attack that Pushed the US to Battle

History Book War
Children's History

Speedy Publishing LLC

40 E. Main St. #1156

Newark, DE 19711

www.speedypublishing.com

Copyright 2017

The Attack on Pearl Harbor took place on December 7, 1941 when Japan's airplanes surprised the United States Navy with an attack on Pearl Harbor, destroying several ships and killing several soldiers. This attack drove the United States to enter World War II. Read further to learn more about the Attack on Pearl Harbor.

WHERE IS PEARL HARBOR LOCATED?

Pearl Harbor can be found on the island of O'ahu in Hawaii. Hawaii is located between Japan and California in the Pacific Ocean. Hawaii was not yet a state during the time period of World War II, but considered to be a United States territory.

Kahuka Point
La'ie
Wahiawa
Wheeler Airbase
Kane'ohe
Kane'ohe Airbase
Pearl City
Harbor
Hickam Airbase
Honolulu
Mamala Bay
Kaiwi Kan

PEARL HARBOR ATTACK

BEFORE THE ATTACK

For two years, WWII had been raging in Asia and Europe, however, the US had not yet entered the war. Japan was attempting to overtake much of Asia and worried about the United States Navy located in Hawaii. In order to stop the US from attacking them, they made the decision to strike.

Japan believed that if they were able to take out the war ships located in Pearl Harbor, the US Navy would then be crippled and never would attack. They were mistaken, however, and the attack resulted in just the opposite. The next day, the United States declared war.

PEARL HARBOR ATTACK SCENE

THE ATTACK

The attack came as a complete surprise as hundreds of Japanese bombers and fighter planes attacked Pearl Harbor. The bombers dropped torpedoes and bombs onto the war ships, as the fighter planes began attacking the US fighter planes while on the ground so they would not be able to take off and fight back. There would be two sets of attacks and by the end of the second attack, several US ships had been destroyed. In addition, the Japanese used submarines, including smaller ones named midget submarines.

JAPANESE NAVAL AIRCRAFT PREPARE TO
TAKE OFF FROM AN AIRCRAFT CARRIER

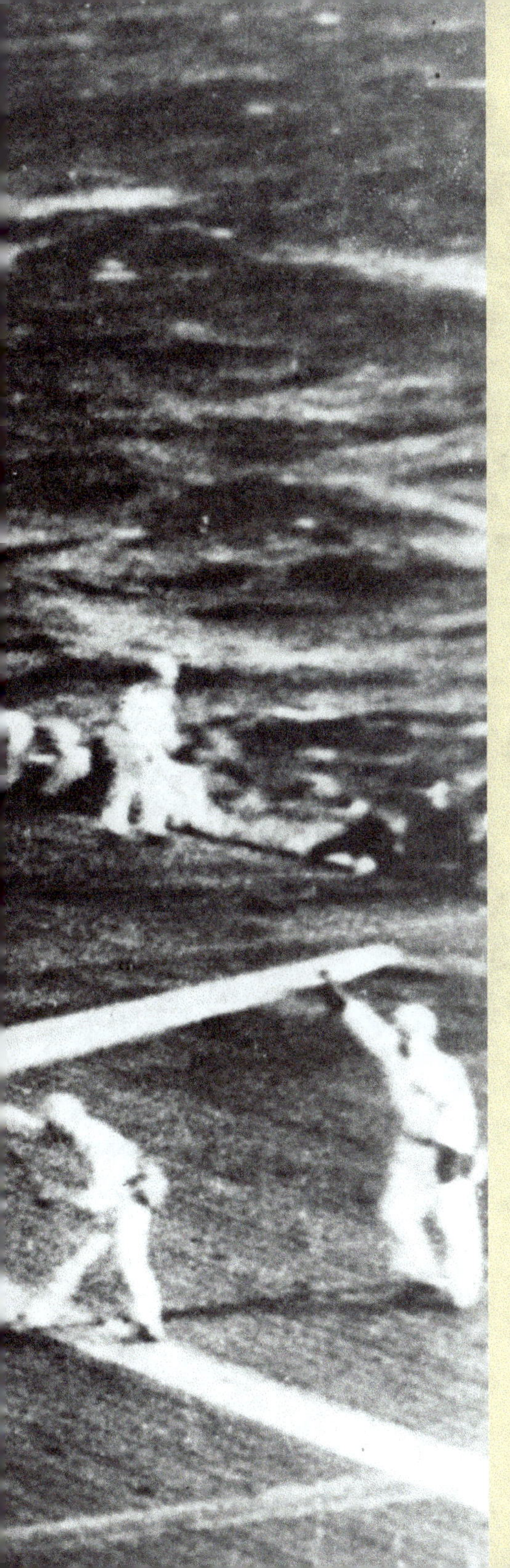

They chose to attack on a Sunday morning, believing the US soldiers would not be as alert. In its entirety, the attack lasted 110 minutes, just short of two hours.

BATTLESHIPS

THE NUMBERS

There were casualties during the attack, from both sides. While Japan had inflicted considerable damage to the United States Navy, they had not crippled it. They did cause damage to several ships, including destroyers, warships and cruisers.

In addition, they destroyed several of the fighter planes and aircraft that were located at the base. All of the US ships but three (the Utah, the Oklahoma, and the Arizona) however, were recovered and used at a later point during the war.

A HELLCAT CRASHES ON USS ENTERPRISE

The sinking of the USS Arizona became the greatest US loss when more than 1,100 US military personnel died when the ship sunk.

USS ARIZONA

DAMAGES AT PEARL HARBOR

In the United States, 2,390 people were killed, including military personnel and civilians. Japan lost 64 people. In the United States, 1,178 people were wounded, including military personnel and civilians. Twelve US ships were sunk or beached and nine were damaged. Five of Japan's ships were sunk or beached. The US had 164 aircraft destroyed and 159 damaged, with Japan having 29 destroyed and 74 damaged.

AFTER THE ATTACK

Citizens of the United States were now in shock. As much as they tried to avoid war, they were not able to overlook this attack. Japan had hopes of breaking the Americans with the attack on Pearl Harbor, but they united them instead.

ncisco News
HUNTS JAPS
PACIFIC COAST
Air Raiders!
WAR EXTRA
ANES NEAR
ATLANTIC!
SAN FRANCISCO
NEWSPAPERS
AFTER PEARL
HARBOR ATTACK

On December 8th, 1941, the following day, the United States proceeded to declare war on Japan.

The Weather
BUFFALO EVENING NEWS
INTER-URBAN
BUFFALO, N. Y., THURSDAY, DECEMBER 11, 1941
FIFTY-TWO PAGES
PRICE THREE CENTS
VOL. CXXIII—NO. 52
Hitler, Mussolini Join Japan In World War Upon America
JAP BATTLESHIP SET AFIRE; LANDING FORCES MOPPED UP
BATTLE ON COAST OF PHILIPPINES IS WELL IN HAND
Consumer Adviser Leaves Post in Defense Agency
U. S. DIDN'T HEED ATTACK WARNING OF KOREAN SPIES
SUMMARY OF TODAY'S DEVELOPMENTS—
Completion of Axis Battle Pact Highlights a World at War
Germany and Italy Fulfill Obligation to Japan; Democracies Discredit Aid It Will Mean to East
CONGRESS READY TO DECLARE WAR ON NAZIS, ITALY
BERLIN, ROME, TOKYO SIGN MILITARY PACT AGAINST U. S., BRITAIN
Duce Tells People That Entire World Is Now Engaged in One Titanic Historical Struggle
Hitler Appears to Have Cold as He Addresses Reichstag; Says Roosevelt Started Conflict
BULLETIN

Germany and Italy, Japan's allies, then declared war on the US three days later. The United States then became a key part of World War II.

AIRCRAFT CARRIER

The US Navy recovered from the attack quickly. There were a number of facilities on the Hawaiian Islands that were not damaged by the Japanese, including repair yards and oil storage depots. In addition, there were no aircraft carriers in Pearl Harbor when the attack occurred. Aircraft carriers soon became the most important navy vessel during the war.

MEMORIAL

There is now a memorial to the United States soldiers that lost their lives during this attack. It is named the USS Arizona memorial and is constructed on the water above the USS Arizona wreckage. This wreckage is now considered to be a US National Historical Landmark.

SAILORS ABOARD
THE NIMITZ-CLASS
AIRCRAFT CARRIER

FRANKLIN D. ROOSEVELT

INTERESTING FACTS

The Japanese reportedly had intended to declare war prior to the attack. However, the message never got to the President.

President Roosevelt gave a famous speech after the attack in which he said December 7th would be a "day which would live in infamy".

Every president since Franklin D. Roosevelt has visited the USS Arizona Memorial site.

The Japanese also used submarines, including smaller ones called midget submarines, in the attack.

The entire attack lasted around 110 minutes, just under two hours.

The Japanese attacked on a Sunday morning because they thought the US soldiers would be less alert at that time.

FORMER NAVY SIGNALMAN 1ST CLASS PAUL
GOODYEAR, RIGHT, A PEARL HARBOR
SURVIVOR AND WORLD WAR II VETERAN

THE WAR IN THE PACIFIC

World War II occurred in two major places which are sometimes referred to as theaters of war. One theater of WWII took place in Europe, and the other took place in the Pacific. Included in the Pacific theater of war were China, Japan, Korea, the Philippines, as well as several other islands and countries located in Southeast Asia.

JAPANESE IMPERIAL ARMY

LEADING UP TO THE WAR

Japan hoped to become a world leader and a strong country. However, since Japan was a small island country, they needed to import several natural resources. Some of its leaders thought they needed to gain additional land by taking over other countries.

HIDEKI TOJO

China was invaded by Japan in 1937. Japan wanted domination over Southeast Asia. Along with Italy and Germany, they aligned with the Axis Powers by signing the Tripartite Pact in 1940. Hideki Tojo, a former General, became Japan's Prime Minister in 1941. He had always been a supporter of Japan aligning with the Axis Powers, and since he was Prime Minister, Tojo now wanted Japan to attack the US.

PEARL HARBOR

While the United States hoped to avoid being involved in WWII, Japan worried that they would attempt to stop them from overtaking some of the countries in Southeast Asia. They then made the decision to attack the US Navy in hopes they would be able to sink enough US ships to keep them from attacking Japan.

PEARL HARBOR SUBMARINE BASE

As discussed earlier in this book, Japan attacked the US Navy on December 7, 1941 at Pearl Harbor. The United States was surprised and several of their ships were sunk by the Japanese. This attack, however, did not end up the way that they had hoped. The next day, the US aligned with the Allies and the attack united Americans along with the objective to defeat the Axis powers, particularly Japan.

THE WAR

Japan moved quickly taking over most of Southeast Asia and by 1942, were on their way to dominance. The US, however, won a crucial battle on June 4, 1942, known as the Battle of Midway. Outnumbered badly, the US Navy was able to sink four of Japan's aircraft carriers and forced them to retreat. This win gave Americans cause for hope and became a turning point during this war in the Pacific.

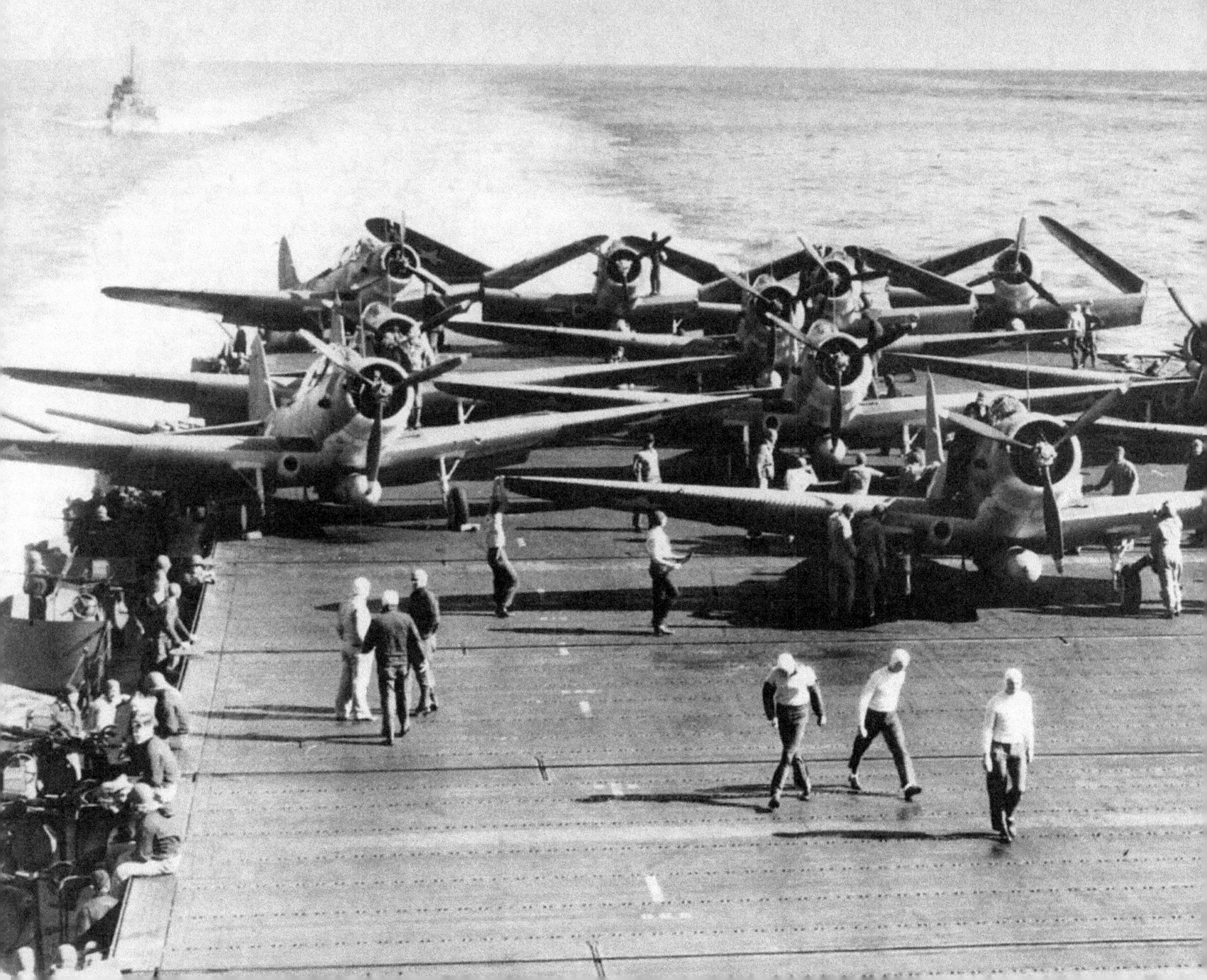

USS ENTERPRISE (CV-6)
DURING BATTLE OF MIDWAY

Following the Battle of Midway, the US started fighting back against Japan, fighting to overtake certain strategic islands located in the Pacific. One of the first battles was for the island of Guadalcanal. Following a fierce fight, the US overtook the island, but learned that fighting Japan was not easy.

There were several battles over islands located in the South Pacific, including Saipan, Tarawa, and Iwo Jima. It took 36 days of battle to take over Iwo Jima. There is now a statue of marines raising a flag on Iwo Jima that has become the Marine Corps Memorial located in Washington, D.C.

AMERICAN ALLIED LEADERS

THE ATOMIC BOMB

In 1945, the Japanese army had finally been forced to return to Japan. The Japanese, however, refused to surrender. American leaders believed that their only option to force them to surrender was to invade Japan's main island. They feared, however, that up to a million US soldiers would lose their lives.

Rather than invading, however, President Truman chose to use a new weapon known as the atomic bomb. The first bomb was dropped on August 6, 1945, on Hiroshima, Japan. It totally destroyed this city and killed thousands upon thousands of people. Japan still refused to surrender. A second atomic bomb was then dropped on Nagasaki, Japan and they would then finally surrender.

BOEING B-29 SUPERFORTRESS BOMBER,
FIRST AIRCRAFT TO DROP AN ATOMIC BOMB
ENOLA GAY
82

EMPEROR HIROHITO

JAPAN SURRENDERS

Japanese Emperor Hirohito declared Japan's surrender on August 15, 1945. It wasn't until September 2, 1945 that the Japanese would sign a treaty of surrender, along with US General Douglas MacArthur on board the USS Missouri. This day was named V-J Day, meaning Victory in Japan.

WAR CRIMES

Japan was guilty of several war crimes during WWII, including the killing of about 20 million Chinese people. This included a policy named "Kill All, Burn All, and Loot All". In addition, they used biological weapons and would torture any prisoners of war. Because of this, several Japanese leaders were executed following the war, including Prime Minister Hideki Tojo.

HIDEKI TOJO LANDS IN MANILA

There is so much more to learn about events leading up to World War II and the Attack on Pearl Harbor as well as events that occurred afterwards. It was devastating for all parties involved.

For additional information, you can visit your local library, research the internet, and ask questions of your teachers, family and friends.

Visit

www.BabyProfessorBooks.com

to download Free Baby Professor eBooks
and view our catalog of new and exciting
Children's Books